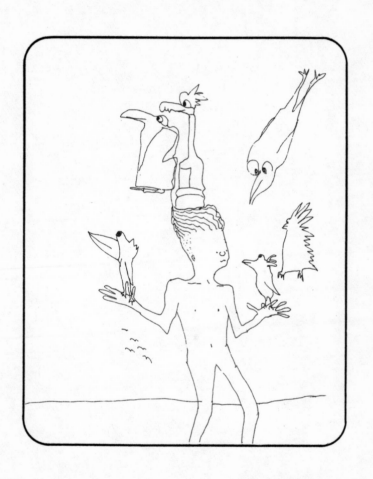

JOHN
LENNON
IN HIS
OWN WRITE

SIMON AND SCHUSTER

New York   1964

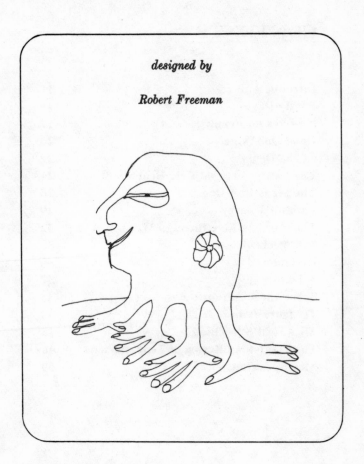

designed by

Robert Freeman

CONTENTS

*Written in conjugal with Paul.

INTRODUCTION

At Woolton village fete I met him. I was a fat school-boy and, as he leaned an arm on my shoulder, I realised that he was drunk. We were twelve then, but, in spite of his sideboards, we went on to become teenage pals.

Aunt Mimi, who had looked after him since he was so high, used to tell me how he was cleverer than he pretended, and things like that. He had written a poem for the school magazine about a hermit who said:
'as breathing is my life, to stop I dare not dare.' This made me wonder right away - 'Is he deep ?' He wore glasses so it was possible, and even without them there was no holding him. 'What 'bus ?' he would say to howls of appreciative laughter.

He went to Quarry Bank High School for Boys and later attended to the Liverpool Art College. He left school and played with a group called the Beatles, and, here he is with a book. Again I think - 'Is he deep ?' 'Is he arty, with it or cultured ?'

There are bound to be thickheads who will wonder why some of it doesn't make sense, and others who will search for hidden meanings.
'What's a Brummer ?'
'There's more to 'dubb owld boot' than meets the eye.'
None of it has to make sense and if it seems funny then that's enough.

Paul

P.S. I like the drawings too.

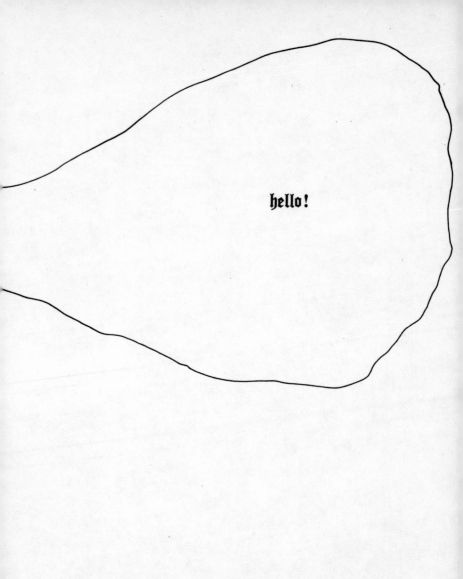

hello!

Partly Dave

There once upon a time was a man who was partly
Dave – he had a mission in life. 'I'm partly Dave' he
would growm in the morning which was half the battle.
Over breakfast he would again say 'I am partly Dave'
which always unnerved Betty. 'Your in a rut Dave' a
voice would say on his way to work, which turned out
to be a coloured conductor! 'It's alright for you.' Dave
used to think, little realising the coloured problem.

Partly Dave was a raving salesman with the gift of
the gob, which always unnerved Mary. 'I seem to have
forgotten my bus fare, Cobber,' said Dave not realising
it. 'Gerroff the bus then' said Basubooo in a voice that
bode not boot, not realising the coloured problem himself really. 'O.K.' said partly Dave, humbly not wishing
to offend. 'But would you like your daughter to marry
one?' a voice seem to say as Dave lept off the bus like a
burning spastic.

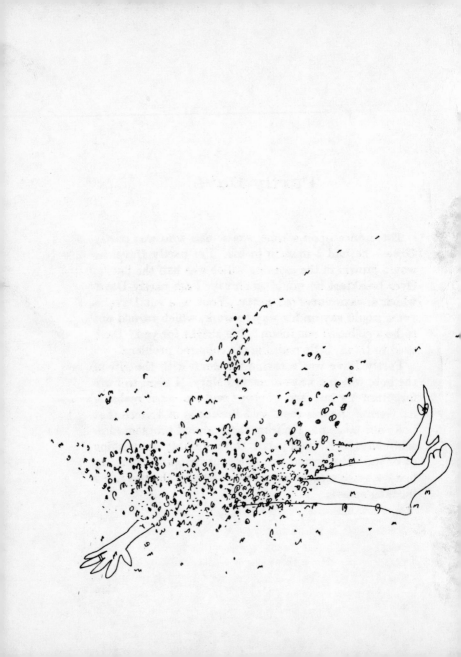

No Flies on Frank

There were no flies on Frank that morning – after all why not? He was a responsible citizen with a wife and child, wasn't he? It was a typical Frank morning and with an agility that defies description he leapt into the barthroom onto the scales. To his great harold he discovered he was twelve inches more tall heavy! He couldn't believe it and his blood raised to his head causing a mighty red colouring.

'I carn't not believe this incredible fact of truth about my very body which has not gained fat since mother begat me at childburn. Yea, though I wart through the valet of thy shadowy hut I will feed no norman. What grate qualmsy hath taken me thus into such a fatty hardbuckle.'

Again Frank looked down at the awful vision which clouded his eyes with fearful weight. 'Twelve inches more heavy, Lo!, but am I not more fatty than my brother Geoffery whose father Alec came from Kenneth – through Leslies, who begat Arthur, son of Eric, by the house of Ronald and April – keepers of James of Newcastle who ran Madeline at 2–1 by Silver Flower, (10–2) past Wot-ro-Wot at 4/3d a pound?'

He journeyed downstairs crestfalled and defective – a great wait on his boulders – not even his wife's battered face could raise a smile on poor Frank's head – who as you know had no flies on him. His wife, a former beauty queer, regarded him with a strange but burly look.

'What ails thee, Frank?', she asked stretching her prune. 'You look dejected if not informal,' she addled.

'Tis nothing but wart I have gained but twelve inches more tall heavy than at the very clock of yesterday at this time – am I not the most miserable of men? Suffer ye not to spake to me or I might thrust you a mortal injury; I must traddle this trial alone.'

'Lo! Frank – thou hast smote me harshly with such grave talk – am I to blame for this vast burton?'

18

Frank looked sadly at his wife – forgetting for a moment the cause of his misery. Walking slowly but slowly toward her, he took his head in his hands and with a few swift blows had clubbed her mercifully to the ground dead.

'She shouldn't see me like this,' he mubbled, 'not all fat and on her thirtysecond birthday.'

Frank had to get his own breakfast that morning and also on the following mornings.

Two, (or was it three?) weeks later Frank awake again to find that there were *still* no flies on him.

'No flies on this Frank boy,' he thought; but to his amazement there seemed to be a lot of flies on his wife – who was still lying about the kitchen floor.

'I carn't not partake of bread and that with her lying about the place,' he thought allowed, writing as he spoke. 'I must deliver her to her home where she will be made welcome.'

He gathered her in a small sack (for she was only four foot three) and headed for her rightful home. Frank knocked on the door of his wife's mothers house. She opened the door.

'I've brought Marian home, Mrs. Sutherskill' (he could never call her Mum). He opened the sack and placed Marian on the doorstep.

'I'm not having all those flies in my home,' shouted Mrs. Sutherskill (who was very houseproud), shutting the door. 'She could have at least offered me a cup of tea,' thought Frank lifting the problem back on his boulders.

Good Dog Nigel

Arf, Arf, he goes, a merry sight,

Our little hairy friend,

Arf, Arf, upon the lampost bright

Arfing round the bend.

Nice dog! Goo boy,

Waggie tail and beg,

Clever Nigel, jump for joy

Because we're putting you to sleep at thr

f the clock, Nigel.

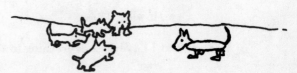

At the Denis

Madam: I have a hallowed tooth that suffer me grately.

Sir: Sly down in that legchair Madam and open your gorble wide – your mouse is all but toothless.

Madam: Alad! I have but eight tooth remaining (eight tooth left).

Sir: Then you have lost eighty three.

Madam: Impossyble.

Sir: Everydobby knows there are foor decisives two canyons and ten grundies, which make thirsty two in all.

Madam: But I have done everything to save my tooth.

Sir: Perhumps! but to no avague.

Madam: Ah! why did I not insult you sooner?

Sir: To late, it must be now or neville.

Madam: You will pull it out for me then?

Sir: No, madman, I will excrete it.

Madam: But that is very painfull.

Sir: Let me see it – Crack! there it be madarce.

Madam: But sir I wished to keep (was anxious to keep) that tooth.

Sir: It was all black and moody, and the others are too.

Madam: Mercy – I will have none to eat with soon.

Sir: A free Nasty Heath set is good, and you will look thirty years jungle.

Madam: (Aside) Thirty years jungle; (Aloud) Sir I am no catholic, pull out all my stumps.

Sir: O.K. Gummy.

The Fat Growth on Eric Hearble

One fat morning Eric Hearble wake up with an abnorman fat growth a bombly on his head. 'Oh crumb,' said Eric Hearble, who was a very very, surprised. Anyway he carried on as Norman for why should he worried? All of suddy he heard a small little voice calling him by name, 'Eric ... Eric Hearble ' it seemed to say though I couldn't say for sure.

That night the very same voice spoke saying 'Eric, I am a growth on your very head, help me, Eric.'

Soon Eric became very attached to his fat growth friend.

'Call me Scab,' the voice said and he was.

'Call me Eric,' Eric said naturly as he could. From then on you never saw Eric without the big fat scab growth on his head. And that's why Eric Hearble lost his job teaching spastics to dance.

'Were not having a cripple teaching our lads,' said Headmaster.

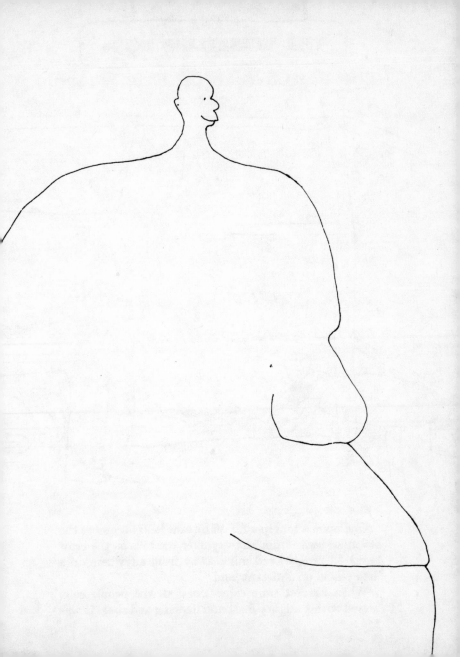

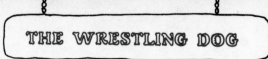

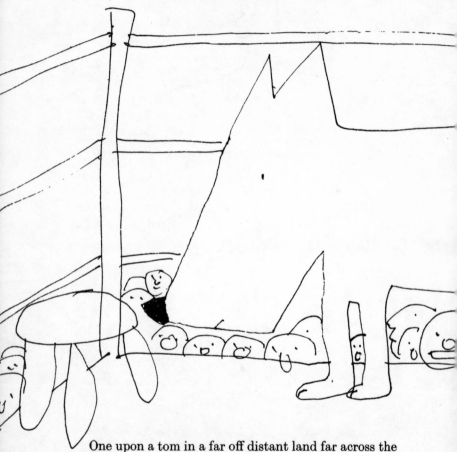

One upon a tom in a far off distant land far across the sea miles away from anyway over the hills as the crow barks 39 peoble lived miles away from anywhere on a little island on a distant land.

When harvest time came along all the people celebrated with a mighty feast and dancing and that. It was

26

Perry's (for Perry was the Loud Mayor) job to provide
(and Perry's great pleasure I might add) a new and
exciting (and it usually was) thrill and spectacular per-
former (sometimes a dwarf was used), this year Perry
had surpassed himselve by getting a Wrestling Dog!
But who would fight this wondrous beast? I wouldn't
for a kick off.

27

Randolf's Party

It was Chrisbus time but Randolph was alone. Where were all his good pals. Bernie, Dave, Nicky, Alice, Beddy, Freba, Viggy, Nigel, Alfred, Clive, Stan, Frenk, Tom, Harry, George, Harold? Where were they on this day? Randolf looged saggly at his only Chrispbut cart from his dad who did not live there.

'I can't understan this being so aloneley on the one day of the year when one would surely spect a pal or two?' thought Rangolf. Hanyway he carried on putting ub the desicrations and muzzle toe. All of a surgeon there was amerry timble on the door. Who but who could be a knocking on my door? He opend it and there standing there who? but only his pals. Bernie, Dave, Nicky, Alice, Beddy, Freba, Viggy, Nigel, Alfred, Clive, Stan, Frenk, Tom, Harry, George, Harolb weren't they?

Come on in old pals buddys and mates. With a big griff on his face Randoff welcombed them. In they came jorking and labbing shoubing 'Haddy Grimmble, Randoob.' and other hearty, and then they all jumbed on him and did smite him with mighty blows about his head crying, 'We never liked you all the years we've known you. You were never raelly one of us you know, soft head.'

They killed him you know, at least he didn't *die* alone did he? Merry Chrustchove, Randolf old pal buddy.

by the light of their faithful dog Cragesmure ...

The Famous Five

through Woenow Abbey

It was holliday time for the famous five by Enig
Blyter; Tom, Stan, Dave, Nigel, Berniss, Arthur, Harry,
Wee Jockey, Matoombo, and Craig? For the past 17
years the fabled fibe had been forming into adventures
on varicose islands and secrete vallets with their famous
ill bred dog, Cragesmure. Their popular Uncle Philpole
with his popular curly white hair and his rugged red
weather battered face and his popular fisherman's boots
and his big junky sweater and his littel cottage.

'Gruddly Pod, Gruddly Pod,' the train seemed to say,
'Gruddly Pod, we're on our hollidays,' and they were.
Pon arrival they noticed a mysterious stranger who bode
no ill?

'Oi what's this 'ere,' he said from behind.

'We're the famous fire by Greenod Bladder,' replied
Tom, Stan, Dave, Nigel, Berniss, Arthur, Harry, Wee
Jocky, Matoombo, and Craig?, and they were.

32

'Don't you dare go on the mysterious Woenow Abbey Hill.'

That night by the light of their faithful dog Crages-mure, they talked Craig and Mtoombo into foing the dirty worj. Soon they were at Woenow Attlee grazine upone an olde crypped who turned round to be the furtive stranger.

'Keep off the grass,' he asked frae a great hat.

Matoombo sprange and soon overpowdered the old crypt with a half helsie. Craig ? quickly fried the old crypt together.

'Wart is the secrete of Woebeat Dobby ?' Craig ? asked.

'Yer can beat me but ne'er ye'll learn the secrete,' he answered from a green hut.

'Anything you say may be used in Everton against you,' said Harry. And it was.

Sad Michael

There was no reason for Michael to be sad that morning, (the little wretch); everyone liked him, (the scab). He'd had a hard days night that day, for Michael was a Cocky Watchtower. His wife Bernie, who was well controlled, had wrabbed his norman lunch but he was still sad. It was strange for a man whom have everything and a wife to boot. At 4 o'clock when his fire was burking bridely a Poleaseman had clubbed in to parse the time around. 'Goodeven Michael,' the Poleaseman speeg, but Michael did not answer for he was debb and duff and could not speeg.

'How's the wive, Michael' spoge the Poleaseman

'Shuttup about that!'

'I thought you were debb and duff and could not speeg,' said the Poleaseman.

'Now what am I going to do with all my debb and duff books?' said Michael, realising straight away that here was a problem to be reckoned with.

I Wandered

On balmy seas and pernie schooners
On strivers and warming things
In a peanut coalshed clad
I wandered happy as a jew
To meet good Doris King.

Past grisby trees and hulky builds
Past ratters and bradder sheep
In a resus baby stooped
I wandered hairy as a dog
To get a goobites sleep

Down hovey lanes and stoney claves
Down ricketts and sticklys myth
In a fatty hebrew gurth
I wandered humply as a sock
To meet bad Bernie Smith

A Letter

Sir,

Why are there not more pidgers and writty about our favourit group (Berneese und zee Rippers). There are thirty-nine of them, you know. We like it cause Alec jumb about and shoes. Pleese send a stabbed undressed envelope of Bern and Ern dancing and doing their splendid to entertain a most deserting group and we hope this fires you as you keeler.

An admirrer.

Afan.

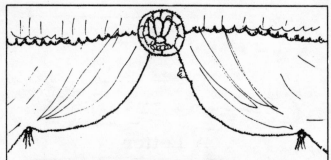

Scene three Act one

(Scene) A broadshouldered room containing hugh fireplace facing a large big windy, a giant-size desk is covered in all type of many business paper and great disorder to look on. There are three or four or five chairs faceing the desk. One are occupied by a scruddy working clog, cap in hook what is gesticulated greatly but humble toward a big fat catipalyst boss. A white man carefully puts coal on the fire and steps back toward a giant door which seems to lead somewhere else. A cat smarting in the corner by the fire leaps up and smiles all on the carpet. A photy of Fieldimarcher Loud Montgammery solving a prodlem looks down on the two men, each of them looking up at it trying to place him.

A dog is quietly gnawing at a pigmy under the giant desk. The time is half past three on the old grandbladder clock by the windy.

Fatty: 'It's harf parst three Taddpill, and the men
             haven't done a strike. Why can't we settle
             this here and now without resorting to a long
             union discussion and going through all that
             bit about your father.'

Scruddy: 'Why don't yer shut yer gob yer big fat get or
             I'll kick yer face in. Yer all the same you rich
             fat Bourgies, workin' uz poor workers to death
             and getting all the gelt and going to France
             for yer 'olidays.'

Fatty: (*going all red and ashen*)

             'But listen Taddpill you're only working two
             hours a day now, and three days a week and
             we're losing money as it is, and here you are
             complaining again about screw screwing and
             I'm trying to help you. We could have built
             our factory somewhere else where men like to
             work, but Ho no here we are goverment-
             sponsored and all that.'

Scruddy: 'Why don't yer shut yer gob yer big fat get
             or I'll kick yer face in. Yer all the same you
             rich fat Bourgies, workin' uz poor workers to
             death and getting all the gelt and going to
             France for yer 'holidays.'

             (*Enter a coloured woman singing a coloured
             song, On her back is a great bundle.*)

Mammy: 'Pope dat barge, left that bail'

             (*She unloads her bundle on the right of the desk.*)

Fatty: (*Impatiently*)

             'What is it Mammy, can't you see I'm haveing
             a prodlem with Taddpill and you come in
             here all black and singing? And get that

   bundle of ruddish away from my big desk!'

Mammy: 'O.K. Kimu sahib bwana, massa'
    (*she lifts the bundle and eats it*)
    'Sho' was naice'

Fatty: 'Anyway what was it mammy?'

Mammy: 'Dat was yo' little daughter, by yo secind
    wife KIMU SAHIB'

Fatty: (*colouring*)
   'But I'm not married, old Mammy'

(*Mammy clasps her hands to her head horryfried*)
   'Oh Lord, I've jes' eaten a bastard!'

(*She runs round the room crossing herself, and singing
another verse. Scruddy stands up replaceing his cap firmly
on his head – walking toward the door he half turns like in
the films and shakes his fist.*)

   'Get this black woman out of this factory
   before the men find out, or yer'll 'ave a strike
   on yer fat Bourgie 'ands. I'm tellin yer that
   fer nothin' yer old bum!'

(*Scruddy walks out of the room leaving Fatty – Mammy
and fourteen little Jewish children all singing together a
kind of hymn.*)

The End

Treasure Ivan

In a little seashore pub in Bristow, a ragged gathering of rags are drinking and makeing melly (before sailing to sea in serge of grate treashy on a sudden Isle far across the ocean).

'Belay there me 'earty scabs,' says Large John Saliver entering. Pegging along towards some old saviours whom have soled the several seas.

'Where be the Parable you normally 'ave on your shoulder, Large John?' Asks Blind Jew looking up.

'Never ye mind' reponds Large John 'And anyways where be your white stick?'

''Ow the 'ell should I know when oi can't see?'

All of a suddy Small Jack Hawkins creep in unobtrugell with a siddy grip on his head.

'Ha ha aa aar Jack lad' says Large John in a typical

42

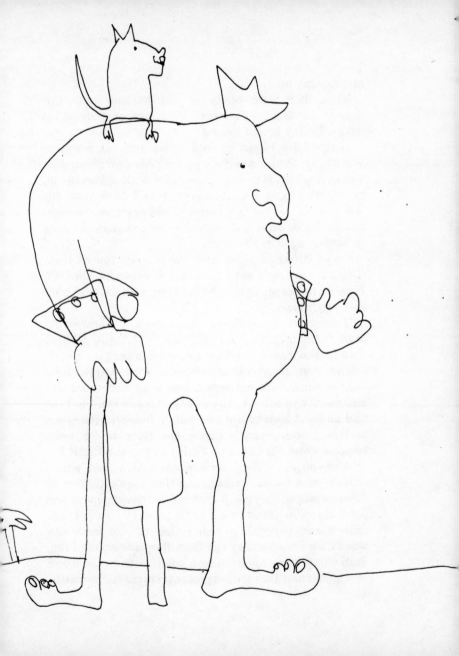

mariner marino.

Soon they were heady fir the harboar with Cpt
Smellit and Squire Trelorgy. That morgan they sailed
with a hearty breeze behind.

Large John began to look upon Jack as a son or
something, for he was ever putting his arm about him
and saying 'Ha Haaaaar', especially with a Parable on
his shouldy. One day, however, Small Jack Hawkins
was just happening in a barret of abbeys when he over-
heated Large John and several other saviours planting
to botany against the Captain.

'Lung Ho' cry a voice from the pidgeon tow on high,
'Lung Ho and alls well!' Yes and it were true – a little
Ivan, cyril carpet agaist the horivan with palmist trees
and cockynuts.

'I wouldn't be suprised if there was not a beardy old
man hobbing from rock to rock.' Thought Disreali
Hands who'd seen the film, and there was.

The first lungboot ashore contained Large John
Saliver Small Jack and some others what were numerous
and sweaty to behold. Anyway they landed on the Ivan
and an owld loon jumps out calling himself Sten Gunn
and he's been living all over the treasure for years
because cruel old Captaive Flint has put the Black Pot
on him and you know what happens with a black pot.

So after a bit of stockade and that they sail home to
Bristow where they're all arrested for development and
Jack Hawkins turns round to be a thirty two year old
midget and Large John Saliver has to pay for a new
woody leg because they run from fireplace on the Ivan.
Sten Gunn turns round to be a young man in the prime
of minister and Tom the faithful cat returns to Newcastle.

All Abord Speeching

1. Speak you Clear and Nasal, for distance.
   'Ron cordially begs to inform Mam all is forgiver.'
   Many peoble express great height with the word
   Mam.

2. Sing you with long voice.
   For discharge
   Deep breathing is Nescafe for a dark voice, deep
   breeding and in haley is very impotent for broad-
   castle and outlying ariels ... visibility nil in Rockall
   and Fredastaire? Practice daily but not if you're
   debb and duff.

3. For sample, the word frenetically wrote, must be
   charged grammactically with bowel pronouned
   strangley.
   eg. *'While talking on you my Ivans are getting cold,
   and you know, as well as I do, that we must strive the
   Ivan while it is hat.'*
   Regarth in Oxfam they speak *'Aivan'* but in Caim-
   bilge *'Oivan'* – the bowel thus strethed pronuned –
   piglo.
   Practice davy but not if your Mutt and Jeff.

THE FINGLETOAD RESORT

OF

TEDDIVISCIOUS

PECKLE AND BRACES (GRANARTHUR)

How many body peoble wash 'Peotle and Plaices'? In a recent Doddipottiddy Poll a roaming retorter intervined asking –

'Do you like Big Grunty better more than Gray Burk'?

To these questiump many people answered

'On the other hand who are we to judge? I mean who are we'?

PANORASTHMA (BBC)

The self same questium was asked through some more kind worjing folk about –

'*Do you prepare Rınkled Dinglebone or Tichie Bimplebean*'?

To this inquest many people answering.

'*Who the hell is Pimpled Dinkletoes? Anyway Who is he?*'

THIS DISPROVES THE PILTDOWN RETORD THAT:

a) Their all washing the rabio.

b) Are their too many adversements on I.T.B.? That seems to be the crutch of the matter. As far as I'm conceived they're foing a grate jobe. But retarding the BBBC's Doddumental Frogrammes – excelent even if they say so theyselfs.

c) $9\frac{1}{2}$ peodle wash I.T.B.

And they wash BBBBC. Every bodypeogle else read the Deadly Excess or the Davey Grail, except Godfree Wind.

Alec Speaking

He is putting it lithely when he says

Quobble in the Grass,

Strab he down the soddieflays

Amo amat amass;

Amonk amink a minibus,

Amarmylaidie Moon,

Amikky mendip multiplus

Amighty midgey spoon.

And so I traddled onward

Careing not a care

Onward, Onward, Onward.

Onward, my friends to victory and glory for the thirtynintl

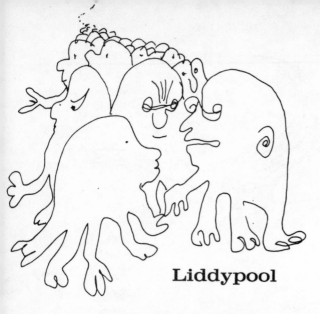

Liddypool

Reviving the old tradition of Judro Bathing is slowly but slowly dancing in Liddypool once more. Had you remembering these owld custard of Boldy Street blowing? The Peer Hat is very popularce for sun eating and Boots for Nude Brighter is handys when sailing. We are not happy with her Queen Victorious Monologue, but Walky Through Gallery is goodly when the rain and Sit Georgie House is black (and white from the little pilgrims flying from Hellsy College). Talk Hall is very histerical with old things wot are fakes and King Anne never slept there I tell you. Shout Airborne is handly for planes if you like (no longer government patrolled) and the L.C.C.C. (Liddypool Cha Cha Cha) are doing a great thing. The Mersey Boat is selling another three copies to some go home foreigners who went home.

There is a lot to do in Liddypool, but not all convenience.

You Might Well Arsk

Why were Prevelant ze Gaute, unt Docker Adenoid getting so friendly? You might well arsk. Why was Seldom Loyled sagged? Why did Harrassed MacMillion go golphing mit Bod Hobe? Why is Frank Cunnings and and the T.U.C. against the Commen Margate? You might well arsk. Why is the Duck of Edincalvert a sailing mit Udda Fogs? Why did Priceless Margarine unt Bony Armstrove give Jamaika away? You might well arsk. Why won't Friendly Trumap give his Captive his pension.

Nicely Nicely Clive

To Clive Barrow it was just an ordinary day nothing
unusual or strange about it, everything quite navel,
nothing outstanley just another day but to Roger it
was somthing special, a day amongst days ... a red
lettuce day ... because Roger was getting married and
as he dressed that morning he thought about the gay
batchelor soups he'd had with all his pals. And Clive
said nothing. To Roger everything was different, wasn't
this the day his Mother had told him about, in his best
suit and all that, grimming and shakeing hands, people
tying boots and ricebudda on his car.

To have and to harm ... till death duty part ... he
knew it all off by hertz. Clive Barrow seemed oblivious.
Roger could visualise Anne in her flowing weddy drag,
being wheeled up the aisle, smiling a blessing. He had
butterfield in his stomarce as he fastened his bough tie
and brushed his hairs. 'I hope I'm doing the right thing'
he thought looking in the mirror, 'Am I good enough
for her?' Roger need not have worried because he was
'Should I have flowers all round the spokes?' said Anne
polishing her foot rest. 'Or should I keep it syble?' she
continued looking down on her grain haired Mother.

'Does it really matter?' repaid her Mother wearily
wiping her sign. 'He won't be looking at your spokes
anyway.' Anne smiled the smile of someone who's seen
a few laughs.

Then luckily Anne's father came home from sea and
cancelled the husband.

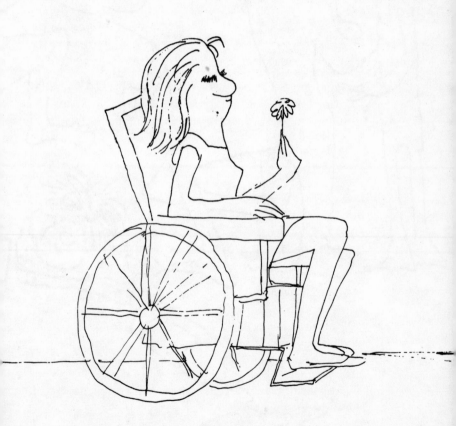

Puffing and globbering they drugged theyselves rampling or dancing with wild abdomen, stubbing in wild postumes amongst themselves ...

Neville Club

Dressed in my teenold brown sweaty I easily micked with crown at Neville Club a seemy hole. Soon all but soon people accoustic me saying such thing as

'Where the charge man?' All of a southern I notice boils and girks sitting in hubbered lumps smoking Hernia taking Odeon and going very high. Somewhere 4ft high but he had Indian Hump which he grew in his sleep. Puffing and globbering they drugged theyselves rampling or dancing with wild abdomen, stubbing in wild postumes amongst themselves.

They seemed olivier to the world about them. One girk was revealing them all over the place to rounds of bread and applause. Shocked and mazed I pulled on my rubber stamp heady for the door.

'Do you kindly mind stop shoveing,' a brough voice said.

'Who think you are?' I retired smiling wanly.

'I'm in charge,' said the brough but heavy voice.

'How high the moon?' cried another, and the band began to play.

A coloured man danced by eating a banana, or somebody.

I drudged over hopping to be noticed. He iced me warily saying 'French or Foe'.

'Foe' I cried taking him into jeapardy.

The Moldy Moldy Man

I'm a moldy moldy man
I'm moldy thru and thru
I'm a moldy moldy man
You would not think it true.
I'm moldy till my eyeballs
I'm moldy til my toe
I will not dance I shyballs
I'm such a humble Joe.

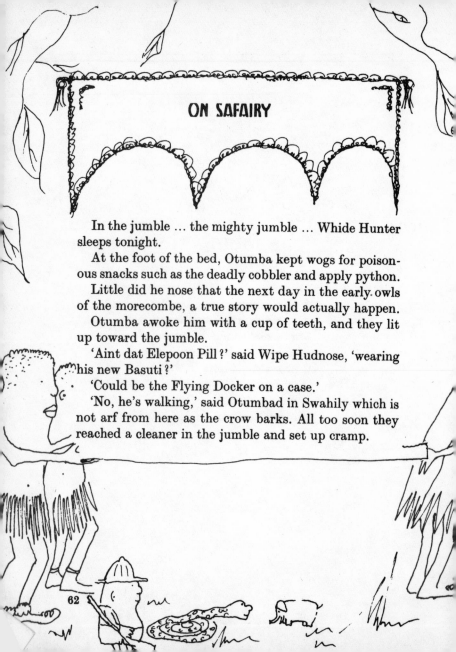

ON SAFAIRY

In the jumble ... the mighty jumble ... Whide Hunter sleeps tonight.

At the foot of the bed, Otumba kept wogs for poisonous snacks such as the deadly cobbler and apply python.

Little did he nose that the next day in the early owls of the morecombe, a true story would actually happen.

Otumba awoke him with a cup of teeth, and they lit up toward the jumble.

'Aint dat Elepoon Pill?' said Wipe Hudnose, 'wearing his new Basuti?'

'Could be the Flying Docker on a case.'

'No, he's walking,' said Otumbad in Swahily which is not arf from here as the crow barks. All too soon they reached a cleaner in the jumble and set up cramp.

WITH WHIDE HUNTER

Jumble Jim, whom shall remain nameless, was slowly but slowly asking his way through the underpants, (underware he was being washed by Whide Hungry.)

'Beat the bus, Otumba,' commanded Wheat Hoover.

'No! but mable next week it will be my turn to beat the bus now standing at platforbe nine.'

Jumping Gym, who shall remain norman, spotted Whit Monday and the Barking Doctorine shooting some rhinostrils and hippoposthumous and Otumbark.

'Stob shouting those animoles.' Bud it hab no inflience upod them. They carried on shotting alligarters, wild boats, garriffes, lepers and Uncle Tom Cobra and all ... Old Buncle Ron Gobble and all ... Bold Rumple, Bom Dobby and all ... Bad Runcorn, Sad Toddy and all.

I Sat Belonely

I sat belonely down a tree,
humbled fat and small.
A little lady sing to me
I couldn't see at all.

I'm looking up and at the sky,
to find such wondrous voice.
Puzzly puzzle, wonder why,
I hear but have no choice.

'Speak up, come forth, you ravel me',
I potty menthol shout.
'I know you hiddy by this tree'.
But still she won't come out.

Such softly singing lulled me sleep,
an hour or two or so
I wakeny slow and took a peep
and still no lady show.

Then suddy on a little twig
I thought I see a sight,
A tiny little tiny pig,
that sing with all it's might.

'I thought you were a lady'.
I giggle, – well I may,
To my suprise the lady,
got up – and flew away.

Henry and Harry

Henry was his father's son and it were time for him to leave school and go into him father's business of Brummer Striving. It wert a farst dying trade which was fast dying.

'But Brummer Striving is a farst dying business, Father,' said young Henry, a young lad. His dad, Harry replied quickly.

'None of thy nonsense, Henry. All thy fathers before-have and before even that before me were Brummers and that's a fact.' With that he pulled his stumps nearer the fire.

'Tell me again father about how you got those prize stumps was it not with a Brummer Towdry?' said young teenage Henry.

'Why do you always ask about my stumps, Son,' said Harry to Henry with a reasurring.

'Because it's a story I love to hear, Father – and besides it's not every one what has a real cripple for a father.'

'There's something in what you say, I dare say,' said Henry eyeing his son proudly; thinking. 'My son's a Brummer if I ever saw one,' and he had.

'I want to be a golfer, Dad,' said Henry hopefully without a laugh.

'You're a Brummer, Son, so get it straight,' said dad Harry.

The next day Henry could not be seen or heard about the quaint little slum and dad Harry was beginning to worry. 'It's not like him, Mother,' he said to a right old hag who was living with them.

'Blast his hide,' said mother, with an accent.

As you might have guessed, teenage young Henry had run around from home and left.

'I'll show that stump,' said Henry to himself, for there was no one with him. Well, it just so happened man that teenage young Henry could not get a golfing job anywhere especially Golfing.

'It seems I'm a born Brummer like dad Harry says I am,' said Harry quietly for no one was listening to him. So he humbled his way homeward like any other teenage Henry would who couldn't get a golfing job. He spotted the slum of his childhood and said out loud 'Crub' which put it in a nutshell.

'Mother, Mother, it's me, teenage young Henry, I'm home,' he said hopeing to be noticed. But hag mother just kept on digging as if she had not noticed him and she hadn't. 'Mother, Mother, it's me' he said repeating himself whilst thinking – 'I wonder what she's digging, it can't be the sounds man.' Still the old wretch kept on digging and also singing to herself – a song you don't often hear now a days. 'Mother, Mother,' said peristant teenage Henry, who was beginning to be a bit of a drag.

'Can't you see I'm burying Soft Harry, your father,' said hag Mother at last.

'All I wanted was a civil answer,' replied Henry assuming responsibility.

Deaf Ted, Danoota, (and me)

Thorg hilly grove and burly ive,
Big daleys grass and tree
We clobber ever gallup
Deaf Ted, Danoota, and me.

Never shall we partly stray,
Fast stirrup all we three
Fight the battle mighty sword
Deaf Ted, Danoota, and me.

With faithful frog beside us,
Big mighty club are we
The battle scab and frisky dyke
Deaf Ted, Danoota, and me.

We fight the baddy baddies,
For colour, race and cree
For Negro, Jew and Bernie
Deaf Ted, Danoota, and me.

Thorg Billy grows and Burnley ten,
And Aston Villa three
We clobber ever gallup
Deaf Ted, Danoota and me.

So if you hear a wonderous sight,
Am blutter or at sea,
Remember whom the mighty say
Deaf Ted, Danoota, and me –
(sometimes we bring our friend, Malcolm.)

A Suprise for Little Bobby

It was little Bobby's birthmark today and he got a suprise. His very fist was jopped off, (The War) and he got a birthday hook!

All his life Bobby had wanted his very own hook; and now on his 39th birthday his pwayers had been answered. The only trouble was they had send him a left hook and ebry dobby knows that it was Bobby's right fist that was missing as it were.

What to do was not thee only problem: Anyway he jopped off his lest hand and it fitted like a glove. Maybe next year he will get a right hook, who knows?

𝕳𝖆𝖑𝖇𝖚𝖙 𝕽𝖊𝖙𝖚𝖗𝖇

(A Play)

Fourteen yearz now I halb been wading for sweet Halbut to return from the wars (little does she know Halbut Hare returbs suddenly to make an honest womb of her.)

H : 'Aim home Rosebeen, from the war y'know.'

R : 'Did yow git thee butter Halbot?'

H : 'Ai've brort ya a negru Rosebeen from the war y'know.'

R : 'For me my very own for me Halbot?'

H : 'Ai was always thinking on you Razebeem my own.'

R : 'Show me this very negru Helbout from the war, this is really living.'

H : 'No'.

R : 'What strange grurth has taken you Halford, am I not your very own?'

Unhappy Frank

Frank looked at the table hardly daring to look at the table.

'I hate that table,' he said 'Bloody owld table in my house.' Then he looked at the clock. 'Damn that clock in my house,' said Frank, for it was his house you know. After a little bit his eye came across his very mother's chair. 'Don't like that chair one bit,' he showbedy. 'Just look at that garbet all filby and durby. How am I supposed to look affaffter all this garby ruddish. Wart am I but a slave tow look upon with deesekfrebit all the peegle larfing and buzing me in front of all the worled. How can I but garry on? How? Hab I no live of my own to do but wart I must ever jub gleenig and looking areftor theese damn owld house of my own?' Frank went over to his dubb old mother, whomn was stikl liffing with him. 'What are you larfing at you dubb owld boot?'

'Havn' I nuff treble without you kakking in the korber?' With that Frank stub up and kicked her plainly on the head. 'Take that for larfing you budd oled griff.' 'I hate that boot,' he said smiling quirkley to themselves.

'I'm going to sell this daft shed and you to aswell, also Mummy.'

So he sold it all and left the country and settled down in another country which he did not like half as much as his dear old home in England with his dear old quaint old luvly mother what he (Frank) lost due to a bad harvest. Which judd go to show what happens.

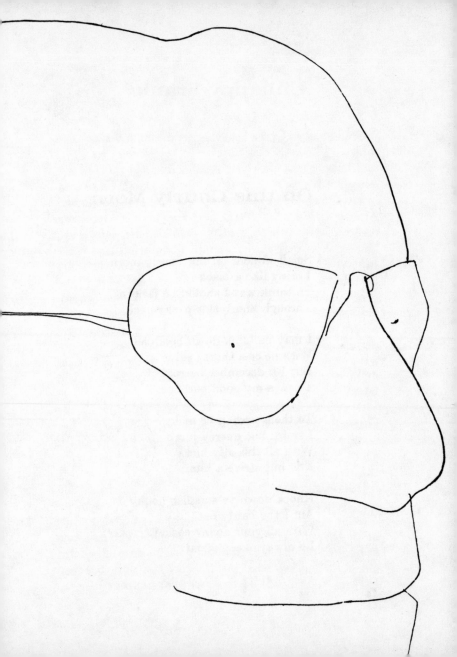

On this Churly Morn

Small wonder on this churly morn
I crivy like a black
To think wot I should be farlorn
Through knorb this packymack

I may be blink down booltoad
With ne'er a thorty skive
But I'll december barrold
To save my good bad Ive

To them perhap be nicky
I smirk but querry jump
With all this alfy hicky
I do but strive a hump

Knock down ye smallish hoqky
Am I the bairly oat?
With all your davey cockey
I'll always keep afloat.

Will I the baggy Dutch man
And haughty bygraves too
To all I give a limpage
To do what they will do.

They rabble till they're tatter
Don't creem the midnight hour
Big Doris flitter flatter
And blacky blackpoo tower

Rephy graun and gratty
Graddie large but smail
She will not brant a fatty
Room to swig a snail

Bilt zeitung dairy apple
Of geltzie sniedypye
Groppy gribble grapple
Varoum the reason why?

Ye bottle ginny derick
And all who sail without
My tall but little Eric
Shall ne'er but cast a clout!

Remplenish thou thy cravie
With all that bodes within
Fall gather barge and davie
The lamb within a bin.

God Speed

It were a small village, Squirmly on the Slug, and vile ruperts spread fat and thick amongst the inhabidads what libed there.

One victor of these gossipity tongues had oft been Victor Hardly, a harmless boot, whom never halmed nobody. A typical quimmty old hag who spread these vile ruperts was Mrs Weatherby – a widow by her first husbands.

'They're holding a Black Matt down at Victors pad,' was oft heard about the village – but I never heard it. Things like this were getting Victor down, if not lower.

'Why but why do they say these bad thing about me when I have but never halmed or speak bad,' he would say, but I never heard him.

'He's drawing bad Christians on the graves,' Mrs Weatherby would spread. The whole village was alarming.

'We can't have all this,' said the Vicar, who was a Christian. 'We'll have to set a trap and catch this fowl fiend what desicated our church.'

Once and forearm plans were made to prove who it were playing the Darryl with the church. On Thursday or Monday a little group of thirty-two people, all dictionaries of the Counsil, and the Parcel and the Vicar all hid noticeably amongst all the other dead things lying about.

'This will catch him, God willy,' thought a man with Oxfam on his face.

After eight hours or so they all noticed that nothing had happened – and they began to wonder – why? after all hadn't they had the information from a reliable sore?

I Remember Arnold

I remember Kakky Hargreaves
As if 'twer Yestermorn'
Kakky, Kakky Hargreaves
Son of Mr. Vaughan.

He used to be so grundie
On him little bike
Riding on a Sundie
Funny little tyke

Yes, I remember Kathy Hairbream
As if 'twer yesterday
Katthy, Kathy Hairbream
Son of Mr. May

Arriving at the station
Always dead on time
For his destination
Now He's dead on line
(meaning he's been got by a train or something)

And so we growt and bumply
Till the end of time,
Humpty dumpty bumply
Son of Harry Lime.

> *Bumbleydy Hubledy Humbley*
> *Bumdley Tum.* (*Thank you*)

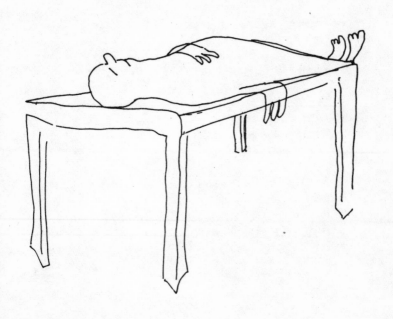